Favorite Charted Designs
by Anne Orr

INCLUDING 119 IN FULL COLOR

Published through the Cooperation of
The Center for
the History of American Needlework
by
DOVER PUBLICATIONS, INC.
NEW YORK

Copyright © 1983 by Dover Publications, Inc.
All rights reserved under Pan American and International Copyright Conventions.

Published in Canada by General Publishing Company, Ltd., 30 Lesmill Road, Don Mills, Toronto, Ontario.

Published in the United Kingdom by Constable and Company, Ltd., 10 Orange Street, London WC2H 7EG.

This Dover edition, first published in 1983, is a new selection of designs from *Laces for Every Use*, Book No. 40, published by Anne Orr, Nashville, Tenn., in 1939; *Needlepoint*, published by Anne Orr in 1938; *J. & P. Coats Centerpieces and Edgings*, Book No. 16, published by J. & P. Coats, Pawtucket, R.I., in 1923; *J. & P. Coats Crochet, Cross Stitch and Tatting*, Book No. 14, published by J. & P. Coats in 1923; *Clark's Designs for Popular Embroidery*, Book No. 17, published by The Clark Thread Company, Newark, N.J., in 1923; *Clark's Designs for Household Linens*, Book No. 11, published by The Clark Thread Company in 1922; *J. & P. Coats Cross Stitch and Crochet*, Book No. 9, published by J. & P. Coats in 1922; *J. & P. Coats Embroidery Monograms, Initials and Handkerchiefs*, Book No. 11, published by J. & P. Coats in 1922; *Edgings, Insertions, Corners and Medallions*, published by Anne Orr in 1917; *Filet Crochet Designs and Their Appropriate Uses*, published by Anne Orr, n.d.

Manufactured in the United States of America
Dover Publications, Inc., 180 Varick Street, New York, N.Y. 10014

Library of Congress Cataloging in Publication Data

Orr, Anne Champe.
  Favorite charted designs.

  (Dover needlework series)
  1. Needlework—Patterns. I. Center for the History of American Needlework. II. Title. III. Series.
TT753.O78   1983   746.44'041   83-8985
ISBN 0-486-24484-9

Introduction

Anne Orr was one of the best-known American designers for popular needlework. Between 1914 and 1945, she published scores of patterns and design booklets, worked for two magazines as an editor, was active in several charities and still found time to raise three daughters and keep a garden. In the early years of the century, when women were still seeking the vote, Orr was a model New Woman, earning a living by combining her art skills and education with the traditionally feminine pursuit of needlework.

Her first patterns appeared in *The Southern Woman*, and were so well received that Orr soon turned to producing books of designs. These sold remarkably well in the years after World War I, and the young designer moved on to a position in the household press that she was to hold for 21 years, as needlework editor of *Good Housekeeping*. She valued good design, and it was her goal that American needle artisans should have resources available to them that would repay the investment of time, labor and materials.

She designed for a variety of media, including knitting, crochet, embroidery, tatting, appliqué and quiltmaking. Orr produced kits for quilts and embroidery, including "Sampler Cards" for children; these were boxed sets of stamped perforated-paper designs with thread and needles, intended to teach youthful fingers the rudiments of counted thread embroidery. Of these media, she seems to have liked best the satisfying block-by-block design of charts, which had been among her first published patterns.

Orr intended her charts to be imaginatively used by the practicing artisan. Charted designs can be used for a great variety of needlework techniques. Cross-stitch embroidery, needlepoint and filet crochet are the three best-known applications, but charts can also be employed in beadwork, weaving, duplicate-stitch on knitting, mosaic crochet, darned-net lace, and "postage-stamp" quilts. Equally endless are the potential end uses: clothing, afghans, towels, bed linens, wall hangings, samplers, doilies, tablecloths, perforated-paper greeting cards, tablecloths, napkins, handkerchiefs, Christmas ornaments, lingerie, baby items and curtains can all be embellished with the graceful and pleasing designs in this volume.

Like many designers, Orr did not work all of the designs herself. A conceptualizer rather than a technician, she employed a staff of needleworkers at her studio to test and make up her patterns before they were marketed to domestic artisans. This division of labor between designer and artisan, much like that between a composer and a performing musician, is an ancient tradition in the needle arts.

From a technical perspective, the original and still-operative rationale for distributing the tasks of design and execution among two or more individuals is that some who are adept at conceptualization may not have equal skill or interest in technical production. Conversely, skilled artisan/technicians may not have a talent or enthusiasm for the labor of design. This is especially applicable in the case of charted designs, in which the limitations of the textile grid make stepped curves necessary and color changes abrupt, both of which pose major challenges to designers. Drafting, color and balance in design are technical areas of expertise in which some training is required. It is these skills that the designer contributes to the needle arts; the engineering processes of execution are the task of the artisan who is equally skilled, but in manual dexterity rather than conceptualization.

Because of these factors, professionally drafted charts and other needlework designs have been popular with working artisans since the rise of the printed book in the sixteenth century. Charts for embroidery, lace and weaving were among the first technical publications of any kind. More than 150 pattern books are known to have appeared in Britain and Europe before 1800, most of them drafted by male designers. This was because, until the second half of the nineteenth century, the necessary training in drafting and art was not available to women. With the establishment of higher education for women, this picture began to change.

The nineteenth century saw for the first time a massive popularization of printed sources on needlework, and a dramatic shift in class restrictions and sex roles in design/execution relationships. To a large extent, these changes were the result of technological developments, both in the commercial areas of printing, transportation, manufacturing and communications, and in the domestic work environments of kitchen and sewing room. Consumer magazines, which were the direct economic result of mass-production methods requiring new marketing and advertising media, were early pioneers in needlework publishing. The most famous household magazines of the nineteenth century were *Godey's, Leslie's* and *Peterson's*, which published designs that continue to be interpreted by modern artisans.

Design publishing for needlework consumers fostered a camaraderie between designers and artisans that had not been possible before books and magazines became less expensive relative to real wages. Furthermore, the publications themselves offered new opportunities to needlewomen. *Godey's* and other nineteenth-century women's magazines had established a precedent for publishing designs by women, breaking with the older tradition of a male professional design priesthood. Reader acceptance of this innovation was so unanimous that by 1894, the male editor-in-chief of *Modern Priscilla* adopted the feminine *nom d'aiguille* "Beulah Kellogg" in order to win the confidence of his readership.

Anne Orr's devotion to the interests of her artisan readers and the popularity of her patterns with needleworkers, are an example of the close relationship that developed between artisans and designs as technological change put pattern books within the economic reach of an increasingly large proportion of home needleworkers.

Economic constraints still, to some degree, limit the number of designs the average artisan can buy. The price of books and magazines has in recent years begun to rise again relative to wages, but many can still be obtained within the needleworker's budget. Dover Publications, in its needlework series, has done much to increase the flow of good designs into the mainstream of American needlework, republishing important out-of-print works at prices that modern artisans can afford. The Center for the History of American Needlework is glad to be involved in this continuing effort.

We would also like to acknowledge the contribution of the historian and publisher, Jean DuBois of La Plata Press, whose research on Anne Orr provided much of the factual information contained in this introduction.

Finally, we express our gratitude to you, the American needleworker, whose desire for fine designs and technical innovation in the textile arts has kept alive the memory of Anne Orr and her sister designers through a half-century of our history.

RACHEL MAINES, PRESIDENT
Center for the History of
American Needlework
Ambridge, Pennsylvania

April, 1982

Afternoon Tea Set

Color Key

▲	CRIMSON
▲	LT. RED
○	STEEL BLUE
◣	YELLOW
	WHITE
■	BLACK
●	DK. MOSS. GREEN
✕	PURPLE

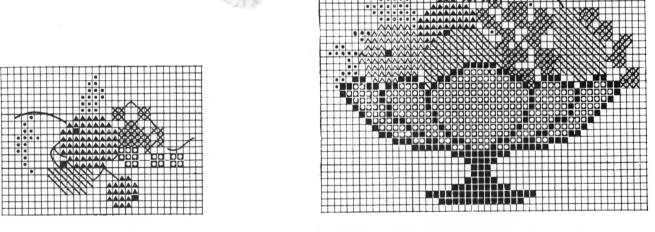

An Unusual Floral Design

Different in arrangement and coloring is the pattern with a cream background and lattice of tan. It is ideal for any use desired and may be made on needlepoint canvas for chairs, stools, etc., or on petit point canvas, 16 meshes to the inch for a bag.

First decide on the size piece to be made, find the center of the canvas and work in this space the floral motif at the upper left of the diagram below. When this has been done, work the straight lines in a soft tone of tan, repeating these all over the canvas, and when this has been finished, it will be found an easy matter to add the flowers and last fill in the background.

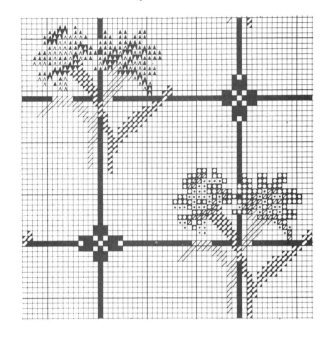

Color Key

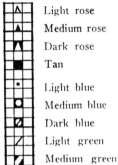

∧	Light rose
▲	Medium rose
▼	Dark rose
■	Tan
·	Light blue
○	Medium blue
∅	Dark blue
/	Light green
⫽	Medium green

5

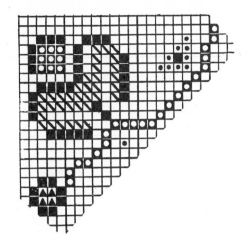

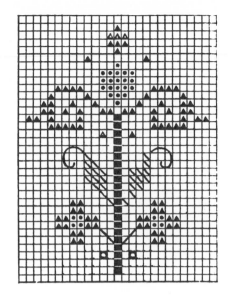

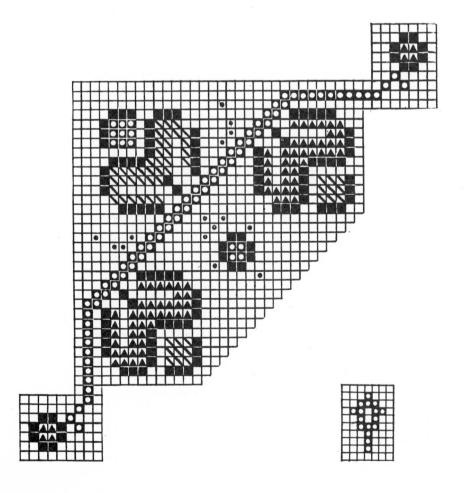

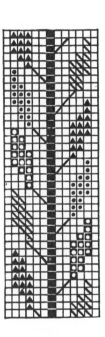

Color Key

▲ yellow

⊡ pink

◨ light green

▨ medium green

◙ dark green

△ red

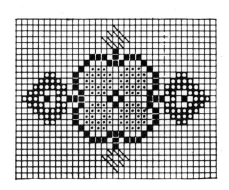

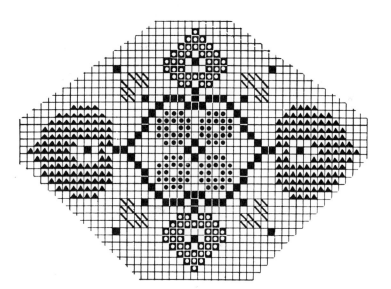

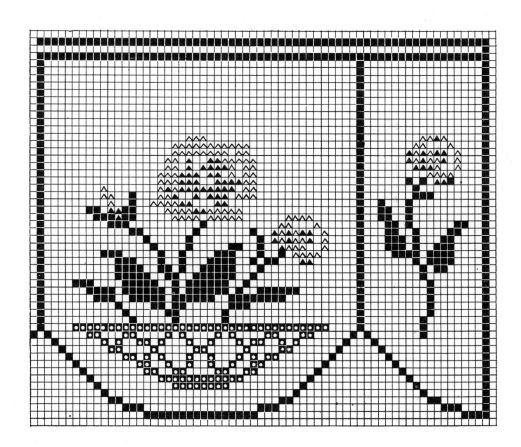

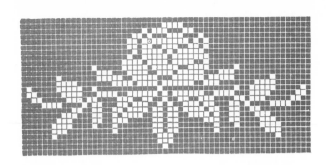

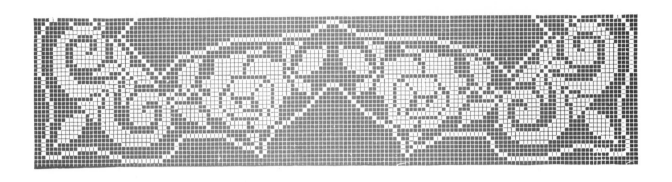

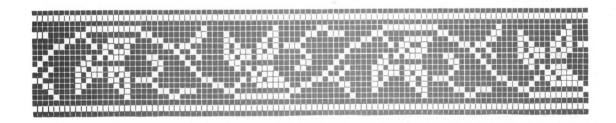

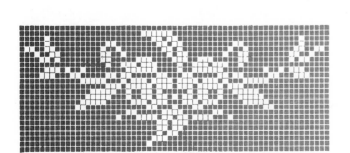

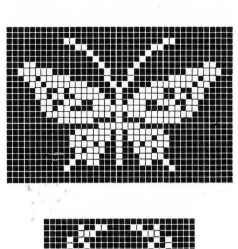

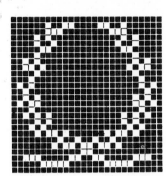

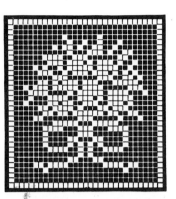

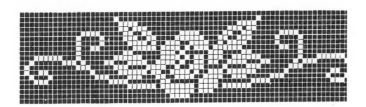

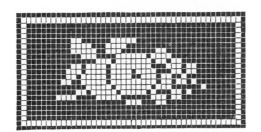

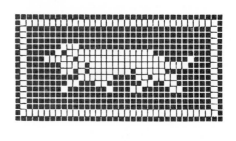

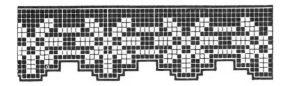

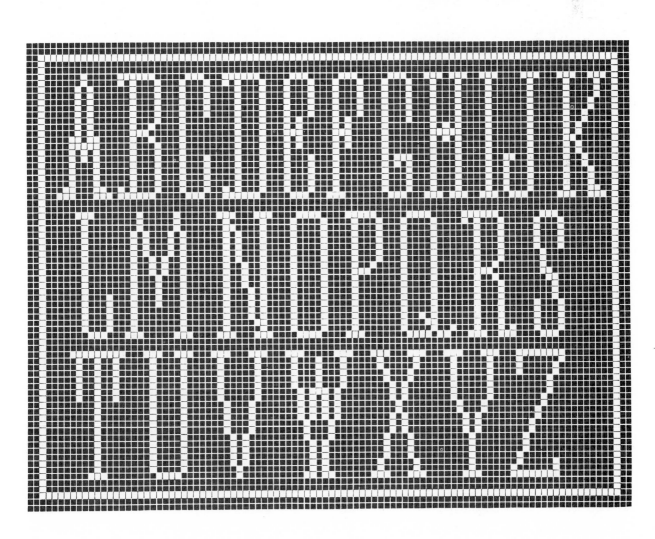

Corner Designs for
Handkerchiefs, Scarves and Napkins

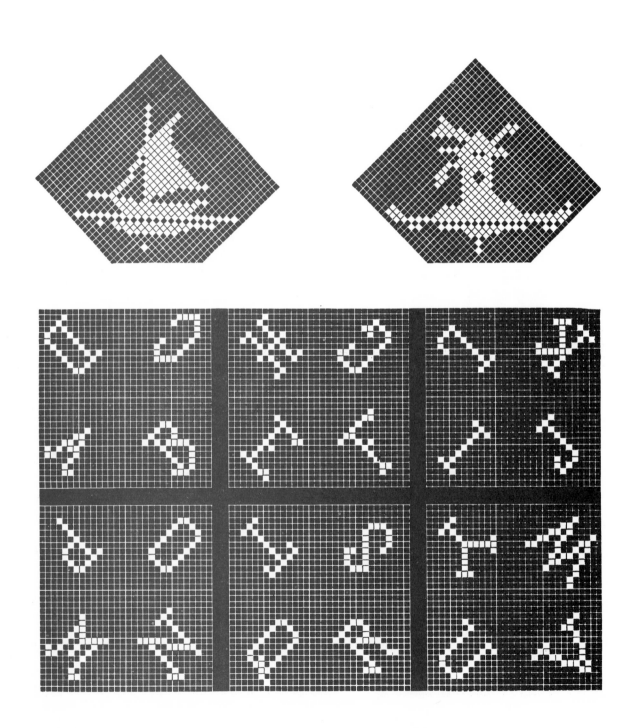

An Italian Runner for Living or Dining Room

This beautiful runner is of loosely woven linen, in a cream color, and is 18 inches wide and 54 inches long. The edge has a narrow hem, and may be rolled or finished with plain or Italian hemstitching. The large design is at both ends and the little motif border goes all around. The entire embroidery is in counted cross-stitch worked through cross-stitch canvas, about 8 mesh-to-the-inch. The cross-stitch canvas must be basted carefully in place on the linen, the cross-stitch worked through canvas and linen (following the pattern below), then the threads of the canvas drawn out. The border motifs and the smaller units of the end design are worked with russet and the lines and the up-and-down diagonal parts of the end design are of golden brown. In the picture of the runner, stitches worked with golden brown show lighter than those worked with russet.

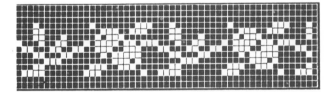

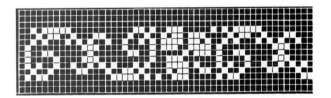

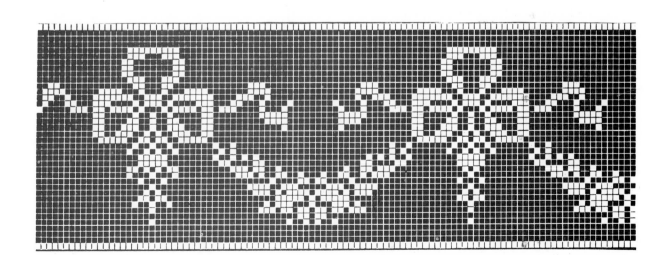

Suggestions for Plate 1

The Fruit Designs Shown as a Corner on
Luncheon Cloth and Napkin.

The parrot design is equally lovely in Petit Point, with six strand floss for a bag; or in cross-stitch or tapestry stitch with tapestry wools, for a screen.

The Twentieth Century ship design is an appropriate decoration for a guest towel, over canvas 16 to the inch, using two strands of embroidery floss. It is very handsome for a bath towel over canvas 10 to the inch, and for a bath rug if over canvas 8 to the inch. The black lines should be outlined with one strand of the six strand embroidery floss, in black.

The fruit design is lovely for a decoration on a afternoon tea or luncheon set. The long spray of fruit at upper right is so arranged that it can be a continuous border or a corner and the latter can be made by turning sheet around and repeating the design as started. The bunch of fruit in left hand corner is useful for medium size pieces, and the apple seems especially appropriate for napkin corners.

A NURSERY SAMPLER

A little "Rain, Rain go away" Sampler may be made as a distinctive decoration for a child's room in that it should carry the name of the child for whom it is made. The worker will find it easy to work the particular name she uses by referring to the small alphabet at the bottom of this page. The design should be worked over canvas measuring 12 to the inch, using three strands of embroidery floss for cross-stitching, and the motto underneath is worked over canvas 20 or 24 to the inch, using one strand of black embroidery floss. The Sampler should be made on cream Italian linen, and when completed, covered with glass and framed with a ½-inch black moulding.

RULES FOR ARRANGING MOTTOES

It is suggested that the worker use her own favorite motto; or if gifted in this way, evolve one from her own brain, so that the Sampler will be more distinctively her own creation.

This can be easily worked, by following the alphabets below and in arranging the letters, follow the simple rule of leaving one mesh or square between every letter of a word, three squares between each finished word, and four between the lines of a verse. Use capitals for the beginning of all lines and important words, and the small letters for the rest of the motto.

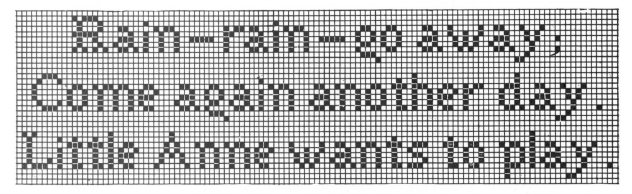

WORKING PATTERN FOR CHILD'S SAMPLER

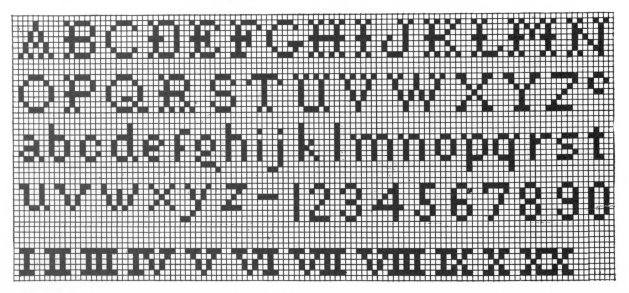

PLATE 1

See page 17 for suggestions.

PLATE 2

See page 17 for suggestions.

PLATE 3

See pages 18–19 for suggestions.

PLATE 4

See page 19 for suggestions.

PLATE 5

See page 19 for suggestions.

PLATE 6

See page 19 for suggestions.

PLATE 7

See page 19 for suggestions.

PLATE 8

Suggestions for Plate 2

The colonial figures on this plate are especially useful because of the interest in colonial furnishings to-day. The two couples at the top of the sheet would be especially charming on either end of a scarf, and for this use should be cross-stitched over canvas measuring 10 to the inch, using three strands of floss. If a set is desired, it is suggested that a couple be placed at one end of the doiley and cross-stitched over canvas 16 to the inch. Such a set should carry a runner the length of your dining room table and 16 inches wide, and doilies to match should measure about 11 x 16 inches. A very pretty finish for such a set is made by turning in a quarter inch hem and catching down with buttonhole stitch made with medium blue floss, or else plain hemstitching with this plain colored thread.

The ladies at tea will be useful in a combination to match this set as the center of a tea cloth, or the ends of a different scarf, etc. Then, they are very lovely as a center design for a dining room Sampler, and under these figures, use the following motto, over very tiny canvas measuring 20 or 24 to the inch with one strand of floss (black):

> Two old friends
> And a cup of tea,
> One of them you
> And one of them me.

The nursery designs on this sheet are appropriate for all linens for the child's use, from aprons and bibs to towels, rugs, etc., and can be made any size according to the size of the canvas over which they are worked.

The old-fashioned coach at the bottom of the page is also delightful for a Sampler decoration, and the following motto is suggested:

> Come to my home
> In an old-fashioned way.
> Come to my home
> And spend the day.

In the case of a Sampler, the finer the stitchery the more beautiful the effect.

For arranging mottoes for Samplers, one will find letters, numerals and directions on page 16.

Suggestions for Plate 3

As one will note, the designs on this plate were particularly planned for the children. They may be used on the rompers, aprons, or dresses as well as on nursery linens.

This is true even of the ship (if worked over a very fine canvas) but it is more attractively placed as the decoration of a Library Sampler. In this latter case it can be worked over canvas measuring 10 to the inch and ½ inch below it, the motto given below is centered and cross-stitched with one strand of black floss over canvas 20 to the inch.

As a Sampler it is very lovely with only the ship and motto framed in a ½ inch wooden frame but a narrow border of 10 to the inch stitchery is very decorative when worked in the same red, blue and black of the ship. Any simple border may be chosen by the worker.

The worker will find great pleasure in adapting these designs to her own needs and arranging a group of them as a decoration for a gift Sampler for a child's room.

For arranging mottoes for Samplers, one will find letters, numerals and directions on page 16.

Motto for Library Sampler

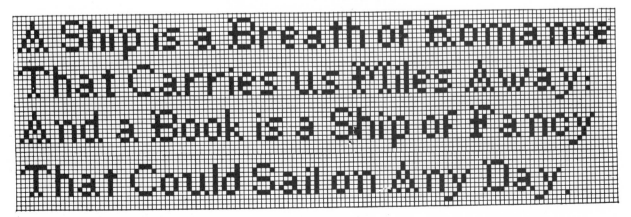

17

Suggestions for Plate 4

This unusual decoration of a table cover is most beautiful in color, as the design for the pattern on Plate 4 will show. Having the embroidery in the center of the material is but another new idea for the needleworker.

The cover should be cut to fit your table. It is made of a heavy oyster colored linen and carries a 2-inch hem which is held down by one or two rows of cross-stitch in black. The design for the border, in peacock feathers, is worked in steel blue, moss green and black; see the charts below. The peacock is worked in light steel blue, moss green, dark moss green, dark willow green, light yellow, yellow, dark yellow, brown, black and the foot and bill are worked in light crimson. The branch of the tree on which he is standing is worked with light golden brown and brown. The cherry blossoms on the tree behind the peacock are worked with light rose, rose and dark rose, centers of light yellow and dark yellow.

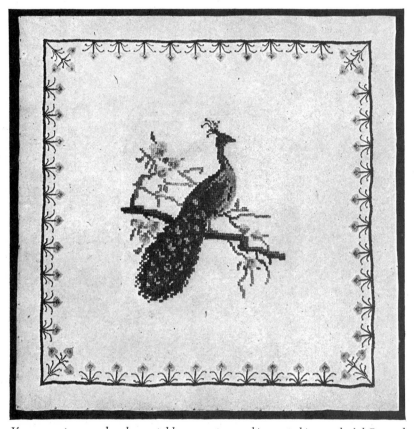

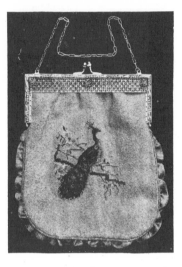

This lovely bag is made in petit-point, either in all-over stitchery or on a dainty gray silk, as shown here. In either case use very fine canvas and six-strand embroidery floss.

If you want a very handsome table cover, try working out this wonderful Peacock.

Border Patterns for Table Cover.

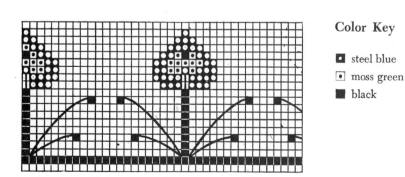

Color Key

- ◨ steel blue
- ◦ moss green
- ■ black

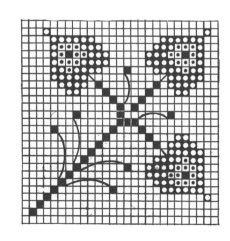

Suggestions for Plates 4-8

The small motifs on these plates are superbly suited for decorating handkerchiefs, scarves, napkins and other household items; they can also be combined to create a Sampler. Combine the rooster, hen and chick on Plate 7 for an interesting and amusing kitchen Sampler; you can use the fruit border at the top of Plate 5 or the cluster of grapes on Plate 8 as the basis for another kitchen Sampler.

Cross-stitch the little girls on Plates 5 or 7 onto counted thread fabric to make a small pillow or wall hanging for a child's room. The borders, edgings and swags on Plates 4–8 can be used to frame any of your needlework designs; these can also be embroidered on strips of counted thread fabric and used for shelf edgings in your kitchen cabinets and closets.

The florals on Plates 4–8 will add a delicate and feminine touch to collars, cuffs and pockets of blouses. Embroider the wreath on Plate 5 onto a pocket; insert your own initial using one of the alphabets on the inside covers of this book.

Nursery Accessories

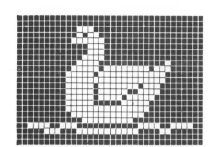

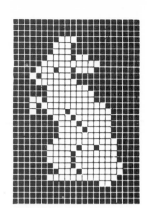

A Dresser Set

DIRECTIONS FOR DRESSER SET

This dresser set is made of scrim, or any other square mesh material, and cross-stitched right over the squares of the material, without use of canvas to work over. The flowers are of Beauty Pink and Rose while the leaves are made of Moss Green and Dark Moss Green as shown in the finished article.

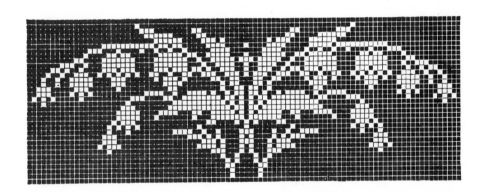

Baskets

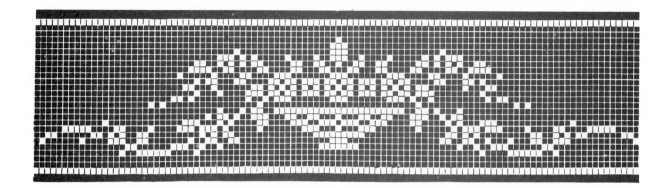

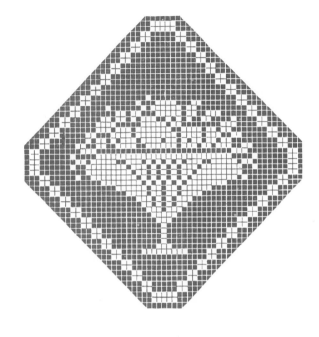

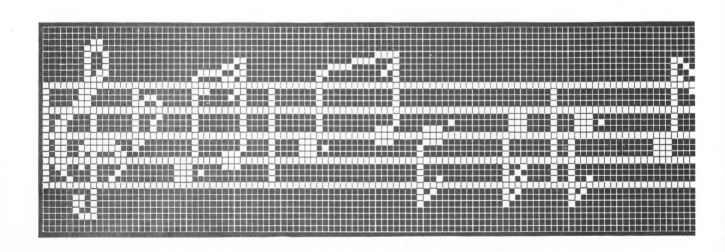